Animal Lifetimes

Written by Keith Pigdon

Series Consultant: Linda Hoyt

WorldWise™
Content-based Learning

Contents

Introduction 4

Chapter 1: What happens in a lifetime? 6

Chapter 2: Starting life 8
How are animals born? 8
Where to lay the eggs? 10

Chapter 3: Growing up 12
Looking after their young 12
Looking after themselves 14
Surviving in numbers 15
How much do animals change? 16

Chapter 4: Being an adult 18
All about breeding 18
How long is a lifetime? 20
How do animals age? 20
Completing the cycle 22

Glossary 23

Index 24

Introduction

All animals have something very important in common – a lifetime! During their lives, all animals hatch or are born, they all find the food they need, they all grow and change, they all make sure that new young of their **species** are born and they all die.

Snakes, dragonflies, elephants and frogs

- What do you know about the animals in the pictures?
- What did they look like when they were born or hatched?
- How long did their parents take care of them?

Chapter 1

What happens in a lifetime?

An animal's lifetime includes all the experiences of an animal from the time it is born until it dies. But as you can see from the table below, different kinds of animals have different experiences.

How is it different for different kinds of animals?			
Kind of animal	Egg or born live?	Does it look after its young?	What do the young eat? Milk or adult food?
mammals	live*	yes	milk
birds	egg	most do	adult food
insects	egg and live	most don't, some do	adult food
fish	egg and some live	most don't, some do	adult food
reptiles	egg and some live	some do	adult food
*Except platypuses and echidnas, which lay eggs			

Thinking like a zoologist

Zoologists are people who study animals. After you have read this book, you can keep track of an animal's lifetime by keeping a journal.

You will need to:

1. Find an animal that you can study. This could be an animal you can **breed** safely at home or in your classroom. You could use silkworms, caterpillars, mealworms, rabbits, hamsters, guinea pigs, some birds such as chickens or canaries, or fish.

Or

You might know of somewhere you can safely watch an animal in the wild without disturbing its breeding cycle.

2. If the animal is in your home or classroom, you need to know how to look after it and what it needs to survive. Food, shelter and cleaning are the important things to find out about.

3. Record information about the changes in the animal's lifetime. When something changes, write the date and what has changed.

4. After the young have become adults, work out how long it was between the main parts of that animal's **life cycle**.

5. Use the Internet to check your records and to find out more about the things you could not see for yourself.

Journal entries

29 April Some bluebirds are making a nest in our birdhouse.

6 May The female bluebird is sitting in the birdhouse most of the time and the male is guarding the house.

22 May The male bird enters the birdhouse when the female leaves to look for food.

29 May The chicks are chirping for food as the parent returns to the nest.

10 July Five chicks have flown from the nest.

17 July Bluebird parents are still feeding chicks in trees around our house.

Chapter 2

Starting life
How are animals born?

All living things start life either as an egg or by being born live. Most mammals and some fish and reptiles are born live. The young grow inside the mother's body.

The time young mammals spend growing inside their mother is called **gestation**. The young grow in an organ called the **womb**. When the young are born, the mother produces milk to feed them.

Turtle hatching

Many animals, however, come from eggs. The adult female produces these eggs, which contain everything needed to form a new animal. All eggs have a shell or covering that protects the new animal growing inside.

Most birds and some snakes use the heat of their bodies to **incubate** their eggs. Incubation keeps the eggs warm and helps the young to develop quickly inside the eggs. When the young have developed, they break out of the eggs. This is called hatching.

What animals come from eggs?
- Birds
- Most fish
- Most reptiles
- Most amphibians
- Millions of **species** of animals without backbones (**invertebrates**), including dragonflies

Interesting incubation
The male emperor penguin incubates its egg on the top of its feet.

How long?
The eggs of some animals such as the dragonfly and the mosquito incubate for seven days. The eggs of other animals such as the freshwater crocodile incubate for 80 days.

For the hamster, gestation can take about two weeks and for the elephant it can take as long as 22 months.

Where to lay the eggs?

Most parents try to make sure their young have a good chance of surviving after they hatch from the eggs. Many parents protect their eggs from **predators** by laying them in a safe place where other animals won't eat them. They might lay eggs in places where there is plenty of food for the **hatchlings**.

Ready-made baby food

Some types of dung beetles make a ball of dung, then lay an egg in the dung. When the egg hatches, the young have a ready supply of dung to eat!

![?]

Did you know?

An egg tooth is essential during hatching. The animal uses it to split the inner membrane and crack the shell of the egg.

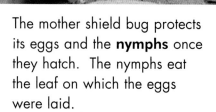

The mother shield bug protects its eggs and the **nymphs** once they hatch. The nymphs eat the leaf on which the eggs were laid.

11

Chapter 3

Growing up

All animals try to make sure that their young have the best chance of survival. Many **newborn** animals are able to look after themselves as soon as they are born. Others, however, need their parents to provide them with food and shelter and to protect them.

Looking after their young

The newborn young of some **species** of animals are completely **dependent** on their parents for much of their early lives. One or both parents provide their young with food and protection until they are old enough to look after themselves.

In the pouch

Young kangaroos grow in a pouch on the mother's stomach. When born, these babies are tiny and undeveloped so the pouch is a safe place for them. They drink their mother's milk while in the pouch.

Leaving the nest

After young birds hatch, parents get food to feed them in the nest. When the young birds are old enough to fly and hunt for their own food, they leave the nest.

Some animals such as lions and elephants live together in groups to care for their young. These young animals learn about the world from their parents. By watching the food their parents eat and reject, the young learn what is safe for them to eat. By watching their mother's fear of particular animals and **environments**, the young discover what animals and places to avoid and how to stay safe. By playing with other animals, the young develop strength and coordination that will help them to defend themselves when they are older.

With the herd

A young elephant looks like its parents when it is born. It drinks its mother's milk for at least the first four years of its life. It also eats plants. The young calf is looked after by other females in the herd, as well as its mother.

Get off my back

Young dugongs drink milk from their mothers. After nearly two years of being carried on its mother's back, the young dugong finally goes off alone.

Looking after themselves

Many animals never see their parents. As soon as they are born, they find food on their own. The female green sea turtle swims thousands of kilometres in the sea to tropical beaches where she digs a hole in the sand to lay eggs which she then covers. By the time the eggs hatch in the warm sand, the turtle parent is far away at sea.

Underwater birth

As soon as it hatches in a pond or stream, the young dragonfly, or **nymph** (left), lives underwater without its parents. It eats insects and small water animals. It has gills for breathing. The nymph can spend as long as four years underwater before it changes into an adult.

Surviving in numbers

Many animals lay a large number of eggs during their lifetimes and have many young. Most of these young do not survive to **breed** themselves. By producing large numbers of young, an animal increases the chances that some of its young will survive to grow up and have their own young.

How many young do they have?				
One young (sometimes more)	**2–4 young**	**5–10 young**	**11–50 young**	**More than 50 young**
dolphin echidna elephant emperor penguin giraffe gorilla horse human koala rhinoceros sheep whale	cheetah grizzly bear leopard lion panda tiger	cat dog	alligator aphid death adder ostrich taipan	green sea turtle 100 spider 50–500 praying mantis 50–2,000 dragonfly 500–800 sea star 3,000 Atlantic salmon 6,000

Did you know?

Most fish produce thousands of eggs to increase the chances of some young surviving. The codfish produces millions of eggs at a time.

How much do animals change?

Young animals have a lot of growing and changing to do before they become adults. Some animals such as young polar bears look just like their parents when they are born, while others don't. But all of them grow to become more like their parents.

Some animals, however, look nothing like their parents. They go through incredible changes before they become adults.

Read about butterflies and the changes they go through before they become adults.

Butterflies

1 Adult butterflies mate.

Polar bear look-alikes

Baby polar bears look like their parents, only much smaller. Baby polar bears weigh about 650 grams – that's about the same as three apples. An adult polar bear can weigh 650 kilograms – that's about the same as a car.

5 Inside the pupa, its body changes until finally a butterfly emerges that can fly, feed and mate.

Where did my skin go?

A dragonfly nymph does not look like its parents. As it grows, the dragonfly nymph sheds its skin about 12 times. When it sheds one skin, it grows another. When it sheds its skin for the last time, an adult dragonfly struggles out of the old skin. Soon its wings harden and it can fly.

2 Butterflies lay eggs.

3 A caterpillar hatches from each egg. Caterpillars feed on plants, grow and **moult**.

4 When the time is right, the caterpillar changes into a different shape called a **pupa**.

Thinking like a mathematician

Make a diagram to show how an animal you know changes and grows during its lifetime.

Chapter 4

Being an adult

All about breeding

When an animal becomes an adult, it can **breed**. Breeding makes sure that the **species** survives. Animal species have many different patterns of breeding. Some breed later in life, some are young when they breed, and some breed only once and then die.

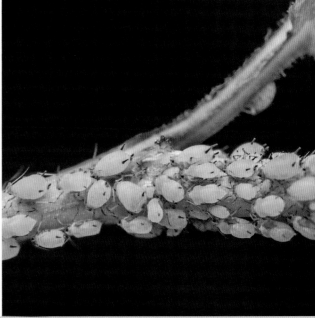

Young breeder

A female mouse starts to breed when it is six weeks old and can have up to ten **litters** in a year with about five to seven babies in a litter. That's up to 70 live babies a year.

Busy breeders

Female aphids can have live female young without mating. They produce ten or more live young a day. These daughters can start breeding in ten days. This means that millions of aphids could be born in a month! Female aphids also mate and lay eggs from which males are hatched.

Salmon travel from the sea to the river where they were hatched to lay their eggs. Many die once they have laid their eggs.

Old breeders

Female green sea turtles can live for 100 years and are over 40 years old before they mate and lay eggs. Each female may lay about 100 eggs in a season. They do this every three or four years. Many of these eggs hatch, although some are eaten by predators. Once they hatch, the young turtles make their way to the sea. Some young turtles are eaten by seabirds, fish and sharks.

How long is a lifetime?

Some animals, such as mosquitoes and other small **invertebrates**, have very short lifetimes. Mosquitoes have been known to complete their lifetime from hatching to breeding and dying in a week.

Mammals, birds and reptiles generally live longer, though the young of these animals do not always make it to adulthood. Many young animals are hunted and killed by other animals, or they die from starvation or disease. Within each species of animal, some individuals live much longer than other members of that species. The table on page 21 shows the record ages for some animals.

How do animals age?

As an animal gets older, its body continues to change. The animal may not be as strong as in its earlier adult life. Some animals begin to move more slowly or with greater difficulty. They might eat less and have more problems caused by diseases. Some animals such as elephants die when their teeth wear out. They can no longer eat so they starve to death.

Looking old
As animals get older, their skin, scales, feathers or fur can change colour or shape. As lions grow old, their fur can get patchy.

How long do animals live?		
	Species	**Age** Oldest recorded in years
Mammals	mouse	3
	guinea pig	7
	rabbit	12
	sheep	15
	dog	24
	cow	30
	lion	35
	zebra	38
	hippopotamus	49
	chimpanzee	50
	horse	52
	elephant	77
	human	122
Birds	swallow	9
	pigeon	35
	goose	80
	vulture	117
Fish	guppy	5
	pike	40
	carp	50
	sturgeon	100
Amphibians and reptiles	small frog	20
	lizard	54
	alligator	60
	giant land tortoise	150
Insects	dragonfly	1
	silverfish	7
	earthworm	10
	queen ant	19

Completing the cycle

Each species of animal has its own **life cycle** that all members of that species may go through. The dragonfly and the elephant have very different life cycles, but what they do have in common is a lifetime.

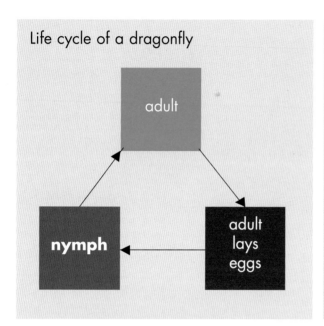

Life cycle of a dragonfly

adult → adult lays eggs → **nymph** → adult

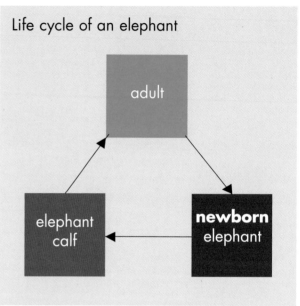

Life cycle of an elephant

adult → **newborn** elephant → elephant calf → adult

Glossary

breed the action of making young animals that are like the parents

dependent needing and relying on another animal to survive

environment all of the living and non-living things in a particular place

gestation the time during which a female animal carries her young inside her body

hatchlings very young animals that have just left their eggs

incubate keeping eggs at the right temperature so they will hatch

invertebrates animals that do not have a backbone

life cycle the stages that all animals of the same species go through from birth to death

litter a number of young mammals that are born at the same time

moult to shed feathers, skin or fur to make way for new growth

newborn animals that are recently or only just born

nymph (larvae) the stage of life of a young insect after it hatches, but before it is an adult

predators animals that kill and eat other animals

pupa the stage of a life cycle when the larva makes a case to live in as it changes into an adult (chrysalis)

species a biological grouping of closely related living things

womb the part in a female mammal's body where the unborn young develop

Index

adults 6, 7, 9, 14, 16, 17, 18, 20, 22, 23

birds 6, 7, 9, 12, 19, 20, 21

breeding 7, 15, 18, 19, 20, 23

diseases 20

eggs 5, 6, 8, 9, 10, 11, 14, 15, 17, 18, 19, 22, 23

fish 6, 7, 8, 9, 15, 19, 21

gestation 8, 9, 23

hatching 4, 5, 8, 9, 10, 11, 12, 14, 17, 18, 19, 20, 21, 23

hatchlings 10, 23

incubation 9, 23

insects 6, 14, 21, 23

invertebrates 9, 20, 23

life cycle 7, 22, 23

live born 6, 8

mammals 6, 8, 20, 21, 23

milk 6, 8, 12, 13

mothers 5, 8, 11, 12, 13

moulting 17, 23

newborn 12, 22, 23

nymphs 11, 14, 17, 22, 23

parents 5, 7, 10, 12, 13, 14, 16, 17, 23

predators 10, 23

pupa 16, 17, 23

reptiles 6, 8, 9, 20, 21

womb 8, 23

young 4, 6, 7, 8, 9, 10, 12, 13, 14, 15, 16, 18, 19, 20, 23

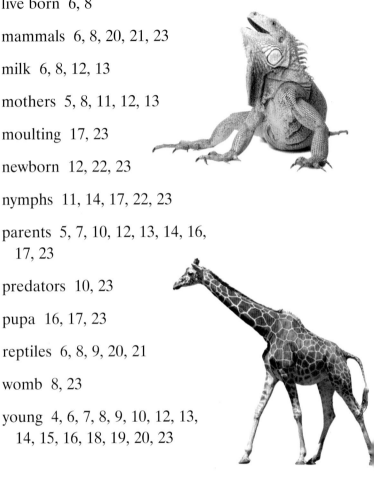